LIVING BEYOND BROKENNESS

Broken Crayons Still Color Devotional

Shelley Hitz

Body and Soul Publishing LLC
P.O. Box 6542
Colorado Springs, CO 80934
www.BodyandSoulPublishing.com

Living Beyond Brokenness / Shelley Hitz. -- 1st ed.
ISBN: 978-1-946118-19-6

Free Gift:

Download free coloring pages and more here:
www.brokencrayonsbook.com

CONTENTS

INTRODUCTION

The Japanese art, Kintsugi, takes broken pottery and repairs it with gold. Instead of discarding it as useless or hiding the damage, they choose to illuminate the repair.

What is your first response to the brokenness in your life?

Is it to discard or hide it? Or do you illuminate the healing God has done in your life and share your story with others?

If you read my book, Broken Crayons Still Color, you know that I have experienced a lot of brokenness in my life.

- Pornography addiction.
- Sexual abuse.
- Murder of my grandma.
- And the list goes on.

But I have also seen the power of God's healing in my life to set me free.

The art of Kintsugi is a powerful picture of how God sees

our broken, imperfect lives.

We tend to see our brokenness as our biggest flaws, mistakes, and regrets. But God can use them to create a masterpiece that will then display His glory.

In this book, I want to encourage you to go beyond the brokenness.

What you see in your life today is not all God has for you. Your broken pieces in God's hands can be restored into something more beautiful than you can imagine.

Are you willing to take the next step with me?

If so, let's go.

YOUR STORY MATTERS

Your story matters.

You have something to share. You have gone through something, however big or small, that can help someone else.

God does not waste anything.

No matter what has been done to you or what you have done, God can take the brokenness of your life and turn it into something beautiful.

Revelation 12:11 says, "They triumphed over him by the blood of the Lamb and by the word of their testimony."

Did you catch that?

We, followers of Christ, triumph over him, satan, by the blood of the Lamb, Jesus, and by the word of our testimony.

We know the sacrifice of Jesus on the cross bought us freedom from our sin. But we don't always think about how much power our testimony has to defeat our enemy.

It is powerful.

And that is why I wrote my book, Broken Crayons Still Color. I shared All. The. Things. in my life that have been painful, traumatic, and difficult.

But I didn't stop there.

You see, with Christ, even if it's not good, it's not the end.

I also shared how God brought healing to my broken heart and freedom to my soul.

I shared my testimony.

And over and over again, I have received emails from readers that say, "Thank you for sharing your story."

First of all, it helps us to know we are not alone. But it also brings hope.

Hope that if I made it through, you can too.

Now it's time for you to do the same. It's time to go beyond the brokenness and allow God to use your life to create something beautiful.

Let's stop comparing and competing against one another and start cheering one another on in the Kingdom of God.

I believe in being honest and sharing my story in an authentic way that lets others know they are not alone. I believe there is always hope.

And I believe that your story matters.

Who will you share your story with today?

 Journaling Prompt

> What tends to stop you from sharing your story of healing and hope with others?

 Prayer

God, I thank you that broken crayons still color. I thank you for all of the ways you have healed me and set me free. Help me to have the courage, as You lead, to share my story of hope with others. In Jesus' name, I pray, amen.

 Godly Affirmation

My story matters.

 Write it out

Write out today's Godly affirmation or Scripture (Revelation 12:11) below.

_____

_____

_____

not
alone

NOT ALONE

E ven when we're in a room surrounded by people, we can feel alone.

I remember feeling alone in first grade. I went to an elementary school in Fort Meade, Florida and most of the kids in my class were children of migrant workers.

They spoke Spanish to each other and I felt like an outsider. I felt alone. I remember longing for just one friend.

However, as we become adults, we can feel alone in our struggles and pain.

Recently, I had a friend on Instagram confide in me that she had a miscarriage. The pain was so deep and her grief was hidden from almost everyone.

When you have a miscarriage, most people don't know what happened, and if they do, they often don't know what to say.

I let my friend know she is not alone.

I, too, have had a miscarriage.

I lost a child early in pregnancy, but the pain was still crushing to my soul. I remember hiking out on a trail by myself so I could scream and cry. I remember crying myself to sleep.

For me, it took over a year to feel "normal" again. I walked through 2014 emotionally numb.

More than anything, I want you to know today that no matter what you are walking through right now, you are not alone.

God is with you and others have walked through similar struggles.

My friend shared this with me, "Thank you, Shelley. I am grateful to God that we are friends and that I felt inspired to tell you. You have been such a strength to me, knowing you have been through this and you are surviving every day. Because we have been through this, we can be God's hands in helping others. I hope one day I can comfort someone as you have for me."

And I was reminded of this Scripture, "He comforts us in all our troubles so that we can comfort others. When they are troubled, we will be able to give them the same comfort God has given us." 2 Corinthians 1:4 (NLT)

We are not meant to walk through this life alone.

We are made for community.

You, my friend, are not alone!

Journaling Prompt

When have you felt most alone?

What is one example of how God is using your previous pain to comfort others?

 *Prayer*

God, thank you that we were never created to walk through this life alone. Please bring the people into my life to encourage me and help me be an encouragement to others. In Jesus' name, I pray, amen.

 *Godly Affirmation*

I am not alone.

 *Write it out*

Write out today's Godly affirmation or Scripture (2 Corinthians 1:4) below.

_____

_____

_____

_____

_____

_____

_____

_____

_____

_____

_____

Show up
AS YOUR
authentic
SELF

SHOW UP AS YOUR AUTHENTIC SELF

Today, I encourage you to show up as your authentic self.

Take off the masks you've been hiding behind and allow your true self to emerge.

Embrace the true you. Embrace the good, the imperfect, and the weird.

Take off the mask of other people's expectations of what you should be and how you should act, the mask of being everything to everyone.

Take off the mask of perfection.

Give yourself permission to just simply be YOU.

For years, I hid behind the mask of other people's opinions. I didn't want to show my authentic self because I thought I would be rejected.

You see, because I don't have children, I often don't fit in with other women my age.

So, I hid.

I didn't think I was worthy of being used by God and assumed that other women would reject me. I didn't think they could relate to me.

However, as I began to shed my false masks and the lies of the enemy, my true self emerged. Who God created me to be started to shine through.

I now know that although I won't always fit in, I belong.

God is using me powerfully as I embrace my authentic self and share my story with others.

And He wants to do the same for you.

The world needs YOU, not who you think you should be, but who God created you to be.

Let God use YOUR unique gifts.

"Having gifts that differ according to the grace given to us, let us use them." Romans 12:6 (ESV)

We are all different. That is our superpower. God didn't make us robots. He created unique individuals with varying gifts and ministries. Now, let's use our gifts.

Amen?

"I don't believe there is one great thing I was made to do in this world. I believe there is one great God I was made to glorify. And there will be many ways, even a million little ways, I will declare his glory with my life." - Emily P. Freeman[1]

Now let's declare God's glory to a world that desperately needs us to show up as our authentic selves.

Let's choose to show up and use the unique gifts God has given us today!

 Journaling Prompt

What masks have you worn? In what ways have you hidden your true, authentic self out of fear of rejection? What are some of the unique gifts God has given you?

 ## Prayer

Lord, thank You for creating me uniquely. Thank You that I am created in Your image and I am fearfully and wonderfully made. Help me take off the masks I wear today and stand confidently in who I truly am. Help me to glorify You with the unique gifts and abilities You've given me. In Jesus' name, I pray, amen.

 ## Godly Affirmation

I am created with unique gifts and abilities.

 ## Write it out

Write out today's Godly affirmation or Scripture (Romans 12:6) below.

_____

_____

_____

_____

_____

_____

_____

_____

_____

_____

not today
shame

NOT TODAY SHAME

Have you ever heard these words before?

You're. Not. Good. Enough.

This is the voice of shame. Shame tells us we're not enough. We're not pretty enough, skinny enough, successful enough, and the list goes on.

It is one of the most common struggles we have today. Never feeling good enough.

In 2002, God set me free from a two-year addiction to pornography. I was free. I was forgiven. And yet, I heard these words loud and clear almost every day.

You're. Not. Good. Enough.

It was the voice of shame.

God had set me free, but shame kept me bound up in the regret of the past. Shame also kept me silent about this part of my life.

I wanted to forget. But God had different plans for me.

On October 9th, 2009, I felt prompted by God to share my testimony on this topic while speaking in front of groups about forgiveness.

I wrote this response in my journal, "I know Lord. I think I've been too ashamed."

I sensed God saying to me, "It's time to stop living in shame about your past and it's time to be real with those who need to hear your story."

And at my next speaking engagement, I obeyed. I shared my story of healing and freedom from sexual sin.

I will be honest.

Even though I'm a different person and now have freedom, it's still hard to share about this part of my life. It hurts and I never know what others will think about me.

So why do I continue to publicly share about the most shameful thing I've ever done?

I think Brennan Manning explains it well,

"In a futile attempt to erase our past, we deprive the community of our healing gift. If we conceal our wounds out of fear and shame, our inner darkness can neither be illuminated nor become a light for others."[2]

You see, every time I share my testimony publicly, there is at least one woman or teen girl that confides in me that she has the same struggle. God is using my story for His glory and to help set others free.

And in doing so, I'm shouting this message loud and clear, "Not today, shame. Not today."

God has created us for freedom.

"It is for freedom that Christ has set us free. Stand firm, then, and do not let yourselves be burdened again by a yoke of slavery." Galatians 5:1

You, my friend, were made for freedom. Fly free today.

 Journaling Prompt

Is there a part of your testimony you haven't shared out of fear and shame of what others will think of you? If so, journal about it below and ask God to set you free today.

 *Prayer*

Thank you, Lord, for your forgiveness and freedom in Christ. Help me to live out that freedom every day. Help me to tell others about your mighty power and what amazing things you have done in my life. In Jesus' name, I pray, amen.

 *Godly Affirmation*

I am made for freedom.

 *Write it out*

Write out today's Godly affirmation or Scripture (Galatians 5:1) below.

_____

_____

_____

_____

_____

_____

_____

_____

_____

_____

_____

beautifully
IMPERFECT

BEAUTIFULLY IMPERFECT

E very day we are bombarded with messages from the media that we need to look, act, and be a certain way.

And no matter how hard we try, we fail miserably at living the "picture perfect" life.

The truth is we can never attain perfection on this side of heaven. We are broken and imperfect.

How would our lives change if we embraced our imperfections and chose to see ourselves as beautifully imperfect every day?

As I mentioned in the introduction, there is a Japanese art called Kintsugi. They take broken pottery and repair it with gold. Instead of discarding it as useless or hiding the damage, they choose to illuminate the repair.

What a powerful picture this is for how God sees our broken, imperfect lives.

The brokenness we see as our biggest flaws, mistakes, and regrets; God can use to create a masterpiece. He uses our lives and our testimonies to display His glory.

"But we have this treasure in jars of clay to show that this all-surpassing power is from God and not from us." 2 Corinthians 4:7

After my miscarriage in 2013, I struggled to exercise consistently. I had gained about 10 pounds and it was not coming off.

Several years later, God revealed that I was neglecting my body because it wasn't doing what I wanted. It didn't bear children and I felt defective. Broken.

So, I prayed for the words God would have me speak over my womb.

I sensed the words, "accepted, loved, healthy, fruitful."

However, there was something else and it wasn't coming to me right away.

Then, I realized it was the word "complete."

I have felt incomplete as a woman because I haven't given birth to children. Tears came to my eyes as I thought about the fact that God sees me as complete.

I am complete. I accept my body the way it is. I am loved, healthy, and fruitful.

I had defined myself as barren for many years. However, I chose to let go of that identity and instead embrace who I am in Christ.

I am beautifully imperfect.

Journaling Prompt

Do you feel the pressure to look, act, and be a certain way? Do you struggle with perfectionism? What area of your life do you need to embrace your imperfections and replace the lies of how you see yourself with the truth of who you are in Christ?

 *Prayer*

Lord, thank you for creating me in Your image. Help me embrace my imperfections and see my brokenness as an opportunity for You to display Your power and beauty. Bring healing to my broken pieces and allow me to see myself through Your eyes. In Jesus' name, I pray, amen.

 *Godly Affirmation*

I am beautifully imperfect.

 *Write it out*

Write out today's Godly affirmation or Scripture (2 Corinthians 4:7) below.

_____

_____

_____

_____

_____

_____

_____

_____

_____

_____

Heir
TO THE
throne

HEIR TO THE THRONE

We need to celebrate who we truly are in Christ.

We are heirs to the throne.

Let that sink in for a minute.

You are an heir with an inheritance waiting for you. This is a big deal.

And yet, so often we live as beggars on the street looking for crumbs when our Daddy, our Papa God, has a feast prepared for us.

I lived much of my life trying to prove that I can survive on the streets instead of thriving in the palace that is ultimately mine.

In third grade, when my grandma was murdered, my life was turned upside down. Everyone at school knew what happened because it was published in the local newspaper. At such a young age, I didn't know how to cope.

I went from being outgoing to not saying more than one or two words to my classmates. I withdrew inside myself and felt like an outsider. I didn't feel accepted.

When I was in fifth grade, we moved to a new school where no one knew about my past. However, I was never the popular one. My sister was the cheerleader and homecoming queen. I was not.

Although I was well-liked, I never felt like I belonged anywhere. I often felt like I was on the outside looking in.

For most of my life, I have tried to prove that I was worthwhile. Although I didn't realize it at the time, I was seeking achievement and accolades for my self-worth. To be seen and to build a name for myself.

As I was journaling about this one day, I sensed God say the following to me. And I believe He is saying the same to you as well.

"You do belong. There is a place for you. No one defines your worth. I do.

It's not about building a name for yourself but simply resting in the name you already have.

My daughter. Powerful Princess. Warrior Princess. Bride of Christ. Heir to My throne.

Because you are my daughter, your name has:

- Authority: even the demons obey the name of Jesus (Luke 10:17).
- Wealth: you have an inheritance beyond what you can think or imagine (Romans 8:17, I Corinthians 2:9-10).

- Connections: brothers and sisters all over the world plus many others (I Peter 5:9).
- Feasts and parties are held in your honor (Luke 15:7, Luke 15:22-24).
- Security: heaven is waiting, the best is yet to come (John 14:2-4).
- Love: a deep unconditional love for generations (Ephesians 3:18-19).
- Good reputation: the name above all other names is Jesus (Philippians 2:9).

Rest in the name you already have. You are mine and I love you."

"Now if we are children, then we are heirs - heirs of God and co-heirs with Christ, if indeed we share in his sufferings in order that we may also share in his glory." Romans 8:17

How do you see yourself? Do you live like an heir to the throne or are you still seeking your worth in other things?

 *Prayer*

Papa God, I thank you that you have adopted me into your family. I am your daughter/son, an heir to Your throne. It is nothing I have done, but it's based on what You have done for me through Jesus Christ. Thank you for giving me a new identity. Thank you that I can rest in the name I already have. I love you. In Jesus' name, I pray, amen.

 *Godly Affirmation*

I am an heir to the throne.

 *Write it out*

Write out today's Godly affirmation or Scripture (Romans 8:17) below.

_____

_____

_____

_____

_____

_____

_____

_____

_____

Pain
INTO
Power

PAIN INTO POWER

D o you know that God can turn your pain into power?

We all experience pain on this side of heaven. We can't avoid it.

But we can choose how we respond to it.

For years, I buried my pain and grief from my grandma's murder somewhere deep inside me.

To be honest, I don't even remember crying after she died. I was only eight years old and didn't know how to process my pain.

However, as an adult, the pain began to resurface. I numbed it through a pornography addiction until God got my attention.

I distinctly remember God saying to me that I was either going to destroy myself through my destructive behaviors or I was going to allow Him to bring healing to the deep places of my heart.

You see, God can transform our pain into power.

It was not an overnight process, but over time the healing came. I finally forgave my grandma's murderer, grieved her death, and allowed God to comfort me.

I believed the lie that if I opened that painful wound in my heart to the Lord for healing, I would never stop crying. I thought I would get stuck in pain and grief forever.

However, the opposite happened.

Yes, I cried. Yes, I screamed. Yes, I felt the anger and pain and grief.

But, eventually, the weight of all I had been carrying for 20 years lifted from me. I felt joy again. And God began to free me from the pornography addiction.

I think we give pain more power in our lives by ignoring it. It festers and grows and we find ways to numb it. We numb our pain through food, shopping, social media, and other addictions.

Whereas when we are willing to honestly look at our past and the painful experiences with the Lord, He can do miracles in our hearts.

If you want more help in this area, I recommend reading my book, "Broken Crayons Still Color," and watching the corresponding videos. I share in detail the healing journey God took me on to let go of the past and begin to heal from the pain.

If you have experienced intense trauma, I recommend talking to a counselor, pastor, or trusted friend who can help you walk through the pain. I worked with a Christian counselor and am so thankful I did.

Always remember that God can turn our pain into power.

What was once my deepest pain has now become my greatest ministry. Will you allow God to transform your pain into power?

"The Spirit of the Sovereign LORD is on me, because the LORD has anointed me to proclaim good news to the poor. He has sent me to bind up the brokenhearted, to proclaim freedom for the captives and release from darkness for the prisoners." Isaiah 61:1

Journaling Prompt

What pain is holding you back today? Ask the Lord for His help to face the pain and allow Him to heal it. Write out what you sense God telling you about your next steps. Then, take the first step today.

Prayer

Lord, I thank you that I can trust you with my pain. Thank you for the hope that healing and freedom is possible. Help me to take the brave steps you are leading me to take today. In Jesus' name, I pray, amen.

Godly Affirmation

God transforms my pain into power.

Write it out

Write out today's Godly affirmation or Scripture (Isaiah 61:1) below.

_____

_____

_____

_____

_____

_____

_____

_____

_____

_____

_____

_____

you have a
CHOICE

YOU HAVE A CHOICE

R ight now, you have a choice.

You can choose to dwell on the past, fear the future, or live fully in the present.

I have always been an emotional person. I cry at the movies and cry when I see others crying.

Therefore, it is easy for me to be swayed by my feelings. However, I have heard it said that although it is important to FEEL our feelings, we don't have to BELIEVE our feelings.

There is a big difference.

Susan David says, "Emotions are data, not directives…We own our emotions. They don't own us."[3]

When we choose to ignore, deny, or numb our feelings, we are susceptible to addictions of all kinds.

I know from experience.

Years ago, I struggled with an addiction to pornography. I realized I was numbing my feelings instead of facing them.

During that season of my life, I learned the power of replacing the lies of the enemy with God's truth. I began to recognize the core lies I believed and wrote out the truth from Scripture to replace each lie on index cards.

I carried these index cards around with me everywhere I went.

When a negative emotion or behavior surfaced, I paid attention. Was there a particular trigger? Was there a specific lie I was believing?

Then, I would take out my cards and re-read them.

Over and over and over, I read these cards.

Some days the cards would be in my pocket, other days in my purse. But they were always close by where I could easily reach them.

And slowly, I began to renew my mind, develop new thought habits, and change my responses.

I realized I had a choice.

I decided to choose to "take captive every thought to make it obedient to Christ" (2 Corinthians 10:5).

Here are a few examples of the lies and truths I wrote out on my truth cards:

Lie: I am afraid of what the future holds.

Truth: God has plans for me—to prosper me and not to harm me, to give me a hope and a future. I can trust Him with my future. He is walking before me, preparing the way. (Jeremiah 29:11; Isaiah 43:18–19)

Lie: I am ashamed of and regret my decisions and mistakes of the past. I can't forgive myself for what I have done.

Truth: I am free from condemnation. I am precious and honored in the eyes of my Father. I value God's opinion of me more than my past or what others think of me. My value comes from being the daughter of the King. (Romans 8:1–2; Isaiah 43:4; Romans 8:15–17)

Lie: I am not worthy of love.

Truth: The Father loves me completely, thoroughly, and perfectly. There's nothing I can do to add or detract from that love. (Isaiah 54:10)

No matter what has been done to you or what you have done, there is hope in Christ.

You are not at a dead end.

You are at a fork in the road.

And today, my friend, you have a choice.

Do your emotions control you? Are you living in the regret of the past or fear of the future? Are you ready to take your thoughts captive and begin replacing the lies of the enemy with the truth from God's Word?

If so, choose one lie and write out the truth to replace it with on an index card or piece of paper. Start carrying that card with you everywhere you go this week. Read it as often as you can.

 ## Prayer

Thank You, God, that I have a choice. My situation is not hopeless, but there is always hope in Christ. Thank You for giving me the power through the Holy Spirit to take every thought captive to make it obedient to Christ. Help me choose to renew my mind with the truth from Your Word. In Jesus' name, I pray, amen.

 ## Godly Affirmation

I have a choice to take every thought captive.

 ## Write it out

Write out today's Godly affirmation or Scripture (2 Corinthians 10:5) below.

_____

_____

_____

_____

_____

_____

_____

_____

_____

_____

_____

_____

LET IT GO

Friends, it is time to let go of whatever is weighing you down today.

Release it. Let it go.

For me, I have had to let go of my expectations of how life should turn out.

I never thought I would struggle with infertility and be one of the few women I know that has never given birth to her own children.

The twists and turns of life.

I have had to let go of other people's opinions.

Some people think I am selfish because I don't have children, while others think I am prideful because I have my own business.

I have learned that the only opinion that truly matters is God's. He sees my heart and knows my motives.

I have let go of trying to control my circumstances and other people.

God is ultimately in control of my circumstances. I am not. Surrendering to His plan for my life instead of trying to force what I think I want always works out for the better.

And the truth is we cannot change other people. Only God can. Amen?

It all comes back to surrender.

But it never comes easy, does it?

It reminds me of the Serenity Prayer.

God, grant me the serenity
to accept the things I cannot change,
the courage to change the things I can,
and the wisdom to know the difference.
Living one day at a time,
enjoying one moment at a time;
accepting hardship as a pathway to peace;
taking, as Jesus did,
this sinful world as it is,
not as I would have it;
trusting that You will make all things right
if I surrender to Your will;
so that I may be reasonably happy in this life
and supremely happy with You forever in the next.
Amen.

- Reinhold Niebuhr[4]

Hebrews 12:1-2 says, "...let us throw off everything that hinders and the sin that so easily entangles. And let us run with perseverance the race marked out for us, fixing our eyes on Jesus, the pioneer and perfecter of faith."

Journaling Prompt

What do you need to let go of today? What is weighing you down?

 *Prayer*

Lord, thank you that because you are in control, I don't have to be. Thank you that I can trust you with the circumstances and people in my life. Thank you that I can let go of other people's opinions and fix my eyes on You. Thank you for helping me to surrender everything that is weighing me down right now. You are a good, good Father, and I love you.

 *Godly Affirmation*

I choose to fix my eyes on Jesus instead of my circumstances or other people.

 *Write it out*

Write out today's Godly affirmation or Scripture (Hebrews 12:1-2) below.

_____

_____

_____

_____

_____

_____

_____

_____

_____

_____

Joy comes IN THE morning

JOY COMES IN THE MORNING

Psalm 30:5 says, "Weeping may endure for a night, but joy comes in the morning." (NKJV)

We all experience pain on this side of heaven. We all have bad days.

But I want to remind you that there is always hope. If it's not good, it's not the end. Joy comes in the morning.

This does not mean we need to pretend everything is okay and deny our emotions. It's about feeling our feelings and allowing ourselves to grieve.

I am an emotional person and for years I didn't know how to process my emotions. And to be honest, I didn't think it would help.

It is incredible how much it helps to let down your guard and give yourself permission to feel your feelings.

Feel them, process them, and then let them go. I have learned that this process brings me to a place of acceptance. Instead of resisting my negative emotions, I deal with them.

Several years ago, I sensed God saying to me that the key to the next layer of my healing was acceptance. A few weeks later, I was at a conference and they talked about the grief cycle.

And I sat there amazed as I saw the final step of grieving on the screen that day.

Acceptance.

According to Elisabeth Kubler-Ross in her book, On Death and Dying, there are five stages of grief and mourning that people from all walks of life universally experience.

1. Denial and isolation
2. Anger
3. Bargaining
4. Depression
5. Acceptance[5]

I had no idea how powerful it would be to apply this same knowledge to my day-to-day emotions.

When something small happens that irritates me, I can now recognize the emotion and process it.

Sometimes I set a timer for 5 minutes to give myself space to cry, scream, complain, get angry, and feel all the things. When the timer goes off, I either give myself more time to process the emotions or I choose to move on. I pray the serenity prayer and ask God to help me accept the things I cannot change.

Acceptance.

Grief comes in waves and so I may have to process my emotions around a particular circumstance or event more than once.

However, my circumstances no longer control me. Through God's help, I feel my feelings and choose acceptance.

And you can do the same.

Journaling Prompt

How do you process your emotions? Are you stuck in the grief cycle about something in your life? It could be something big or small. Journal about it and give yourself space to feel your feelings. Then, ask God for His perspective on the situation.

 *Prayer*

God, thank you for my emotions. Thank you for your promise that joy comes in the morning. Today I choose to feel my feelings and process them with You. I give myself permission to grieve and ask that You help me let go of the emotions weighing me down today. Instead of resisting my feelings, I choose the road that leads to acceptance. Help me travel this path today. In Jesus' name, I pray, amen.

 *Godly Affirmation*

I give myself permission to feel my feelings and process them.

 *Write it out*

Write out today's Godly affirmation or Scripture (Psalm 30:5) below.

_____

_____

_____

_____

_____

_____

_____

_____

when life Gets blurry

ADJUST your focus

WHEN LIFE GETS BLURRY, ADJUST YOUR FOCUS

What is your first response when you receive bad news?

Do you say, "OH NO!" and panic? Do you immediately go into victim mode and cry out, "Why me??"

I tend to react emotionally with panic and easily slip into feeling like a victim of my circumstances.

However, I want to respond like Psalms 112:7-8, which says, "They will have no fear of bad news; their hearts are steadfast, trusting in the Lord. Their hearts are secure, they will have no fear; in the end, they will look in triumph on their foes."

We can choose to be reactive to our circumstances or we can be proactive.

This is a concept Stephen Covey writes about in his book,

"The 7 Habits of Highly Effective People."[6]

A reactive person allows circumstances they can't control to determine their behavior. If the weather is terrible, they are in a bad mood. They blame outside circumstances for their performance. This can lead to the victim mentality.

On the other hand, a proactive person will take full responsibility for their life. Instead of focusing on the circumstances they can't control (the weather, economy, other people's opinions, etc.), they focus on what they can do in each situation.

The best part?

We have the freedom to choose our response.

We can choose to be reactive or to be proactive. We can choose to focus on what we can't control or we can take personal responsibility for our lives and focus on the things we have influence over and can change.

For much of my life, I have been a reactor. I have allowed my circumstances to jerk my emotions up and down. If I got good news, my day was great. However, when I received bad news, I would immediately panic and get stuck in fear.

Yes, we still need to feel our feelings. Yes, we still need to face the facts.

But we have a choice.

When life gets blurry, and we receive bad news, we can choose to adjust our focus.

Journaling Prompt

Are you reactive or proactive when you receive bad news? What circumstances are currently out of your control? What can you choose to focus on instead?

 *Prayer*

Thank you, God, that You are in control. I admit that I want to be in control, but I realize many circumstances are out of my control today. I choose to surrender those circumstances into Your capable hands and focus instead on what I can do. Help me be proactive when I receive bad news. Help me to have your peace no matter what comes my way today. In Jesus' name, I pray, amen.

 *Godly Affirmation*

I have no fear of bad news. My heart is secure.

 *Write it out*

Write out today's Godly affirmation or Scripture (Psalms 112:7-8) below.

_____

_____

_____

_____

_____

_____

_____

_____

_____

_____

comparison

IS A

liar

COMPARISON IS A LIAR

For most of 2019, comparison whispered in my ear that I was a failure as a business owner and CEO.

As I watched my friends' businesses take off and celebrated their successes, I felt confused and wondered why God was not bringing me the same kind of success.

Comparison told me it wasn't fair, I was doing something wrong, and ultimately, I was not enough.

However, things changed when I went out to run on a clear blue-sky day in Colorado in November. There was snow still on the ground from a snowstorm earlier that week. But that didn't stop me.

And on that run, I had a breakthrough.

God revealed to me that comparison is ALWAYS a liar.

First, He prompted me to look up the facts and check our business finances for this year compared to last year.

I took out my phone and logged into our accounting

software to run the reports. Although we still had two months left of the year, our business was already ahead of where we were for the entire previous year.

So even with all the ups and downs, we were still moving forward.

God also reminded me that His main goal for me this year was to improve my health. I have been on a health journey this year and have come so very far.

In the area of my health, I have had a lot of success. Whereas some of my business friends had not improved in the area of health or in some cases even declined over the last year.

When I was comparing their success in business to mine, I felt like a failure. But God showed me that was not the whole story.

Beware of comparison.

It always whispers in your ear lies that can lead you into stinkin' thinkin' and never feeling good enough.

One of the things God has continued to say to me repeatedly this year is to take my eyes off of other people and fix my eyes on Him. The journey He has for me is unique and won't look like anyone else's.

But, it's good.

Even when I can't see the results I think I should have, God is always at work.

On my run that day, I sensed God saying how very proud He was of me. Tears formed in my eyes and a huge weight lifted off my shoulders.

No matter what you have accomplished this day, this week, this month, or this year, He is saying the same thing to you.

He is so proud of you.

Your value is not dependent on what you accomplish but on who you are.

Let's kick comparison to the curb today. Comparison is a liar.

"A flower does not think of competing to the flower next to it. It just blooms." Zen Shin[7]

"And let us run with perseverance the race marked out for us, fixing our eyes on Jesus, the pioneer, and perfecter of faith." Hebrews 12: 1b - 2a

In what areas have you been comparing your life to others? Are you comparing their highlight reel to your blooper reel? Have you felt pressured to do things others are doing even if it's not what God is asking you to do right now?

 *Prayer*

Thank you, God, that my value is not dependent on what I accomplish but instead based on who I am in You. Thank you for reminding me today that comparison is a liar and I don't have to listen to it. I choose to let go of comparison today so that I can fix my eyes on You and hear Your voice. Many times, the journey You have for me won't make sense at the time but I choose to put my trust in you regardless of my circumstances. I love you. In Jesus' name, I pray, amen.

 *Godly Affirmation*

I am free from comparison as I fix my eyes on Jesus.

 *Write it out*

Write out today's Godly affirmation or Scripture (Hebrews 12: 1b – 2a) below.

_____

_____

_____

_____

_____

_____

_____

_____

_____

_____

CONCLUSION

God has more for you. He is inviting you to go beyond the brokenness in your life.

As you recognize the enemy's lies and begin to replace them with God's truth, amazing things will happen in your life.

Just like Kintsugi, where the broken pieces are repaired with gold, God will begin to heal your brokenness and display His glory to the world through your life.

Let's recap what we learned together.

1. My story matters. (Revelation 12:11)
2. I am not alone. (2 Corinthians 1:4)
3. I am created with unique gifts and abilities. (Romans 12:6)
4. I am made for freedom. (Galatians 5:1)
5. I am beautifully imperfect (2 Corinthians 4:7)
6. I am an heir to the throne. (Romans 8:17)
7. God transforms my pain into power. (Isaiah 61:1)
8. I have a choice to take every thought captive. (2 Corinthians 10:5)
9. I choose to fix my eyes on Jesus instead of my

circumstances or other people. (Hebrews 12:1-2)

10. I give myself permission to feel my feelings and process them. (Psalm 30:5)

11. I have no fear of bad news. My heart is secure. (Psalms 112:7-8)

12. I am free from comparison as I fix my eyes on Jesus. (Hebrews 12: 1b – 2a

My prayer is that you will take these truths from Scripture and allow them to transform your life.

Then, use the process for replacing the enemy's lies with God's truth and apply it to each area of brokenness in your life.

In doing so, you are allowing God to shine through your life as the "gold" that holds everything together.

I am praying for you and I'm in this with you.

CJ AND SHELLEY HITZ

CJ and Shelley Hitz enjoy sharing God's Truth through their speaking engagements and their writing. On downtime, they enjoy spending time outdoors running, hiking and exploring God's beautiful creation.

To find out more about their ministry or to invite them to your next event, check out their website:

www.ShelleyHitz.com

Note from the Author: Reviews are gold to authors! If you have enjoyed this book, would you consider reviewing it on Amazon.com? Thank you!

Free Gift:

Download free coloring pages and more here:
www.brokencrayonsbook.com

NOTES

[1] Emily P. Freeman, A Million Little Ways: Uncover the Art You Were Made to Live, (Ada, MI: Revell, 2013), 40.

[2] Brennan Manning, Abba's Child: The Cry of the Heart for Intimate Belonging, (Colorado Springs, CO: NavPress, 2015), 12.

[3] "The Gift and Power of Emotional Courage" TedWomen video, published November 2017, accessed May 25, 2021, https://www.ted.com/talks/susan_david_the_gift_and_power_of_emotional_courage. Time stamp 12:37 - 12:59.

[4] "Serenity Prayer" Wikipedia.org, published March 1, 2004, accessed May 25, 2021, https://en.wikipedia.org/wiki/Serenity_Prayer.

[5] Elisabeth Kubler-Ross, On Death and Dying, (New York, NY: Scribner, 1969).

[6] Stephen R. Covey, The 7 Habits of Highly Effective People, (New York, NY: Simon & Schuster, 1989), 79.

[7] Zen Shin quote, published on Goodreads, accessed May 25, 2021, https://www.goodreads.com/quotes/1135747-a-flower-does-not-think-of-competing-to-the-flower